JOHN LEWIS

CIVIL RIGHTS CHAMPION AND POLITICIAN

"When you see something that is not right,
not fair, not just, you have to speak up.
You have to say something;
you have to do something."
⌐ John Lewis ¬

BY GOLRIZ GOLKAR

Published by The Child's World®
1980 Lookout Drive • Mankato, MN 56003-1705
800-599-READ • www.childsworld.com

LIBRARY OF CONGRESS CATALOGING-IN-PUBLICATION DATA
ISBN 9781503854468 (Reinforced Library Binding)
ISBN 9781503854949 (Portable Document Format)
ISBN 9781503855328 (Online Multi-user eBook)
LCCN: 2021930453

Printed in the United States of America

Cover and page 4 caption:
John Lewis in 2009.

CONTENTS

Chapter One

SEPARATE AND UNEQUAL

When the Civil War ended in 1865, slavery in America was finally over. Formerly enslaved African Americans celebrated their newfound freedom. They were eager to begin new lives as equals to whites. But they would soon discover that freedom did not mean equality.

A family of formerly enslaved people on the porch of their house in 1874.

Black workers taking a break in St. Louis, Missouri in 1890.

In the South, strict new laws were put in place. These laws told African Americans how and where they could work and live. Sometimes it seemed like slavery had not ended at all. Black people did not have the same rights as whites. They earned less money and were often forced to work cheaply for white employers. Many whites did not see African Americans as equals. They did not want to interact with them. Eventually, more laws were created to separate the two **races**. In schools, churches, buses, and most every public place, African Americans were completely **segregated** from whites. Even in the North, African Americans were treated poorly. While segregation laws never officially existed there, African Americans still had limited work opportunities and faced **racism** every day.

After the Civil War, the South enacted laws called Black Codes. These laws denied Black people equal rights. While the codes were different in each state, overall they deeply affected the way all Black people lived. Housing, employment, property ownership, and voting were all affected by these codes.

Segregation laws stated that Black and white people would be separate but equal. For Black Americans, equality did not exist. They might have won their freedom, but they were not free to live as they wanted.

A Black man takes a drink from a water cooler labeled for "colored" people in Oklahoma City in 1939.

Equality would not come for many more decades. It would take the courage of people, both Black and white, to make it happen. For John Lewis, the fight for **civil rights** would take blood, sweat, and tears.

When Lewis was born in Alabama in 1940, slavery was long over. Still, he was the **descendant** of slaves. He was the son of poor farmers who worked for a white landowner. Segregation was the only life Lewis had ever known. From an early age, Lewis knew he wanted to end segregation and **discrimination** against Black people. He believed they deserved equal rights. He worked hard on his family's farm. He studied well in school. He treated everyone, no matter their beliefs, with respect.

"IF NOT US, THEN WHO? IF NOT NOW, THEN WHEN?"
JOHN LEWIS, 1941

John Lewis in 2016 under a quote of his that is displayed in the Nashville Public Library.

The young boy from Alabama would be beaten, insulted, and jailed many times throughout his life. But he would never back down. He would become one of the "Big Six" leaders of the **civil rights movement.** He would participate peacefully in many important protests. He would live a long life as a respected **activist** and politician who helped create more equal laws. He would pave the way to a better life for African Americans. He would bring Black and white people together in peace.

John Lewis would fight fiercely for civil rights. Yet he would never hold a weapon. He would never raise his fists. He would use the power of his voice.

Chapter Two

A "PREACHER" IS BORN

John Robert Lewis was born on February 21, 1940, in Troy, Alabama. He was the third of ten children. His parents were **sharecroppers** who worked on a white man's farm. When they raised enough money to buy their own farm, John started helping them.

During the harvest season, he would leave school to help his family pick corn, cotton, and peanuts. Even after they bought their farm, the Lewis family remained very poor.

Lewis in 1963

John's family went to church every Sunday. John loved listening to the preacher's sermons. These powerful speeches inspired him to be a good person. They also showed him it was possible to be an African American leader. Since southern laws segregated Black and white people, John attended an all-Black church. His preacher inspired the churchgoers with messages about faith and **resilience** when life was hard. At home, John began preaching his own sermons to the farm's chickens. He loved to read to them from the Bible. John's parents called him the "Preacher." Little by little, John was finding his voice.

Schools for Black children, like this one in Alabama, were often in poor condition.

John started to ask questions about his life. He could not understand why segregation existed. He went to school with only Black children. Restrooms, restaurants, parks, and other public places had separate areas for Black and white people. Signs that read "Whites only" and "Colored only" divided these areas around town. John's parents told him to just follow the rules and stay out of trouble.

John tried to listen to his parents. At school, he loved to read. His favorite teacher in elementary school encouraged him to read as much as he could. When he was 16 years old, he decided to get a membership card at the public library. He went there with other kids

A police officer places a segregation sign in front of the Illinois Central Railroad in 1956.

from his family. But when they got there, they were turned away. The library was for whites only. John was heartbroken.

Rosa Park's booking photo after she was arrested.

Rosa Parks was often called the mother of the civil rights movement. After the success of the Montgomery bus boycott, she lost her job and was harassed by whites. Still, she continued to support civil rights events. She moved to Detroit, where she worked as a secretary for a Congressman. With her activist husband, she started an organization to help young people in Detroit live better lives.

John was not the only African American who was getting tired of segregation. During that time, a massive **boycott** was happening in nearby Montgomery, Alabama. Several months earlier, a Black woman named Rosa Parks had refused to give up her bus seat to a white man. Parks was arrested and forced to pay a fine. The Black community was outraged. They decided to protest by not riding the bus. This would cost the city of Montgomery lots of money. The boycott lasted for a whole year. In the end, the protesters won. The bus system was finally desegregated.

John read about the boycott in the newspapers. He was fascinated by the power of African Americans banding together. He also listened to a well-known leader, the minister Dr. Martin Luther King Jr., speak on the radio. Dr. King preached about civil rights. He urged other African Americans to continue protesting peacefully.

John was empowered by Dr. King's words. In 1957, he applied to Troy State College. The college only admitted white students, but John wanted to attend. He received no answer. Frustrated, he chose a small Black college in

A crowd cheers for Martin Luther King, Jr. after a court appearance in 1956.

Nashville, Tennessee. He began training to become a minister. But he could not keep quiet about his troubled thoughts.

After moving to Nashville, he wrote Dr. King a letter. He described how he had wanted to attend a white college. He thought it was unfair that he had not been given a chance.

John knew his parents wanted him to stay out of trouble. But maybe some trouble would be worth it. He was ready to take action. It was time to join the fight for civil rights.

Chapter Three

A BUDDING ACTIVIST

John settled in Nashville and began his studies. He joined a group called the Nashville Student Movement. These activists believed they could put an end to segregation through peaceful protests. Not long after arriving in Nashville, John received a reply from Dr. King. John's letter had impressed him. He asked John to visit him in Alabama during a school break.

When John saw Dr. King, the minister offered to help John **sue** the college for discrimination. However, Dr. King warned him that his family would be endangered. Some people would be angry about a Black person challenging segregation. John would need his parents' permission first. In any case, Dr. King encouraged him to keep fighting for civil rights.

Lewis speaks at a meeting in 1964.

John's parents were afraid to sue the college. They asked John to stay in Nashville and accept life as it was. John agreed to forget the lawsuit. However, he would not accept life as it was.

When John returned to Nashville, he got to work. He and the other activists decided to organize **sit-ins** at white-only lunch counters. Activists in other southern states were organizing sit-ins as well. In February 1960, John participated in his first sit-in. When asked to leave, the activists quietly refused. They were insulted and attacked. But they did not fight back. John remained seated until he was arrested.

Lewis being arrested in 1964 following a protest in Nashville.

John's parents learned about his arrest. They were ashamed of their son. But John was proud. He believed that these peaceful protests could end segregation. Over the next six years, he would be arrested 40 times during protests.

Over the next three months, John and the other activists staged more sit-ins around downtown Nashville. They were beaten, insulted, and arrested over and over again. Not once did they turn violent. In May 1960, protest leaders and store owners finally came to an agreement. Six stores agreed to open their lunch counters to African Americans. John and his friends had made history. Nashville became the first southern city to begin desegregating public places. The activists knew they had won only a small battle. They needed to keep fighting.

A sit-in at a lunch counter in Nashville in 1960.

In 1961, John participated in one of the most famous civil rights protests. It was called the Freedom Rides. In 1946, the Supreme Court had declared segregation on interstate buses and trains **unconstitutional**. In 1960, they added that all areas linked

A group of Freedom Riders stand at the door of a bus in Birmingham, Alabama in 1961. Drivers refused to take them.

to interstate travel—such as restrooms and bus terminals—must ban segregation. But everyone knew that segregation existed in the South. A civil rights organization named CORE decided to test these rulings. They wanted to send an **interracial** group of activists on bus rides in the South. The Black and white activists would ride side by side.

By then, John had finished his religious training and become a minister. He was now a college student at Nashville's Fisk University. While his education mattered to him, his activism did as well. Since John had been involved in the Nashville protests, he was one of 13 activists chosen as a Freedom Rider. He put his studies on hold and joined the protest.

The Freedom Riders' bus after the mob attack in Alabama.

In May 1961, the Freedom Riders left Washington, DC in two buses. They would be traveling to New Orleans, Louisiana. When they arrived in South Carolina, John and another rider were beaten. The violence worsened when they reached Alabama. In the city of Anniston, a mob set fire to the first bus. They beat the Freedom Riders as they escaped the burning vehicle. When the second bus arrived, the mob attacked its passengers as well. The second bus still continued to Montgomery. At the bus station there, the riders were viciously attacked with bats and other objects. John was beaten unconscious. Eventually, the Freedom Riders completed their journey to New Orleans by airplane. Dr. King demanded that the government protect the activists from the mobs. The police were always arriving late. They usually did not stop the attacks. From newspaper front pages to TV screens, the violence was on full display. Both Black and white people were being savagely beaten.

The 13 brave Freedom Riders inspired hundreds of others to participate in more Freedom Rides over the next few months. By November 1961, the government had officially banned segregation for interstate travel.

Many people thought the Freedom Riders were heroes. John Lewis was especially admired. No matter how many times he was beaten or jailed, he never gave up or turned violent. Dr. King was especially impressed. He remembered the boy from Troy who had wanted to fight for civil rights. John was about to get his biggest chance of all. Up until then, he had been protesting quietly. Soon, thousands of people would get to hear his voice. The preacher had much to say.

Some of the people who harmed the protesters were members of the Ku Klux Klan, or KKK. After the Civil War, some former Confederate war veterans formed this group to carry out violent acts against African Americans and white people who helped them. The KKK was responsible for numerous acts of violence and deaths during the civil rights era and beyond.

Lewis and fellow Freedom Rider James Zwerg after being beaten in Montgomery.

Chapter Four

MARCHING TOWARD EQUALITY

After the success of the Freedom Rides, John was recognized as a civil rights leader. In 1963, he became the new chairman of the Student Nonviolent Coordinating Committee (SNCC). The interracial civil rights group had participated in sit-ins and the Freedom Rides. John was the perfect leader for the group's peaceful protests. With his new title, he became one of the "Big Six" leaders of the civil rights movement. He decided to leave college to devote more time to activism.

In August of that year, the U.S. government prepared to vote on civil rights laws. The Big Six leaders decided to assemble together in Washington, DC. They wanted to speak up for civil rights. On August 28, 1963, John joined the other leaders at the March on Washington.

Lewis speaking at a meeting in 1964.

Dr. King's empowering speech moved the peaceful crowd of over 250,000 people. He spoke of his dream to see equality for all. When it was John's turn to speak, the tone shifted. While he also spoke of hope and equality, John delivered a powerful message about the need for society to work together. He preached that patience was not the answer to discrimination. African Americans wanted their freedom immediately and would not stop until they had it. With every word he spoke, the crowd cheered wildly. At just 23 years old, John was already inspiring others.

Dr. Martin Luther King Jr. gave his famous "I Have a Dream" speech at the March on Washington. In his speech, he described his dream to see African Americans become equals to whites and for discrimination to end.

In July 1964, the U.S. government passed the Civil Rights Act. With this new law, discrimination against people of any race, religion, or **ethnicity** was banned. This meant that segregation in public places was finally illegal. It was a major victory. However, John and other activists knew that African Americans were still not treated

Lewis and Martin Luther King, Jr. talk with reporters after meeting with President Kennedy in 1963.

as equals. While the new law was supposed to give Black citizens stronger voting rights, officials in the southern states found ways to prevent Black people from voting. They were often given **literacy** tests, charged fees, or even beaten if they tried to vote.

Lewis being beaten on Bloody Sunday, 1965.

Earlier that June, John and other civil rights leaders had tried to help African Americans register to vote in Mississippi. They had mostly failed. Many activists—both Black and white—had been tortured or killed. The federal government had done little to help the activists. The Civil Rights Act did not stop the violence either. Some African Americans began to question if they should fight back when attacked. For John, violence was never the way.

Instead, he began fighting for equal voting rights. Between 1963 and 1964, Dr. King had taken hundreds of African Americans to the courthouse in Selma, Alabama. He wanted them to register to vote. Each time, they were denied.

On March 7, 1965, John joined Dr. King in leading 600 peaceful protesters in a march from Selma to the state capitol in Montgomery. When the protesters reached the Edmund Pettus Bridge in Selma, they came face to face with state troopers blocking their path. The local sheriff demanded that the protesters break up their crowd. The protesters stopped marching, but they stood still in silence. What happened next was one of the most violent attacks of the civil rights movement. Cheered on by white crowds standing nearby, the troopers began spraying the protesters with tear gas. Many troopers beat the protesters with sticks and whips. One trooper came after John. With a heavy blow from the trooper's club, John's skull was fractured. He would become an important face of this "Bloody Sunday."

The event was shown on television. Millions of Americans, both Black and white, were horrified by what they saw. John's family watched in terror as their loved one was attacked brutally. They were afraid he would end up dying for civil rights.

Many Americans stood up for the protesters. They wanted to know why the marchers had not been protected. They could not believe that police officers had been allowed to attack American citizens. In over 80 cities, protesters assembled in support of the Selma activists.

In addition to John Lewis and Dr. King, the "Big Six" consisted of four other important civil rights leaders. Whitney Young helped improve the lives of urban Black people through better housing and education. A. Philip Randolph dedicated his life to organizing Black people's jobs. James L. Farmer Jr. was the director of CORE. Lastly, Roy Wilkins worked as executive secretary of the NAACP—the biggest and oldest civil rights organization in America.

President Lyndon B. Johnson condemned the violence. One week after Bloody Sunday, he met with Congress to discuss passing the Voting Rights Act. Under this law, African Americans would no longer experience legal discrimination at the polls. They would not have to take literacy tests, and they would not be segregated from whites. The law passed by August that year. The following year, poll taxes were also banned in all elections.

Millions of African Americans were finally able to register to vote in the South. It was another major victory for civil rights.

In just under a decade, John had become one of the most well-known leaders of the civil rights movement. African American voices were finally being heard. With every vote, they spoke their minds. Slowly, they gained a voice in government as well. The preacher was not done speaking just yet.

Chapter Five

A NEW CAREER IN POLITICS

In 1966, John left the SNCC. The organization wanted to become more aggressive in the civil rights fight. But John still wanted to fight peacefully. He decided to return to his studies at Fisk University. In 1967, he graduated with a degree in philosophy and religion. Around this time, he met a librarian named Lillian Miles. Lillian was also passionate about justice and civil rights. In 1968, John and Lillian married and settled in Atlanta, Georgia. They adopted their only child, John-Miles, in 1976.

Lewis speaking in 1975

In 1970, John became the director of the Voter Education Project. The project helped civil rights groups raise money to educate and register African Americans to vote in the South. In 1977, John decided to leave the Voter Education Project and run for Congress. He believed that a government role would give him an even greater chance to make a difference for civil rights.

While John lost the election, he still won a new position. President Jimmy Carter chose him to lead ACTION, a federal agency that managed volunteer programs. As their leader, John was in charge of overseeing human rights missions carried out by volunteers around the world.

John and Lillian Lewis on election night in 1986.

In 1981, John was elected to the Atlanta City Council. As a councilman, he spoke up about the need for values in government. He worked hard to improve Atlanta's neighborhoods by cleaning up old buildings and constructing new schools. In 1986, John decided to run for Congress again. This time, he won a seat in the House of Representatives. He was elected as a Democrat representing Georgia's Fifth Congressional District, including all of Atlanta.

As a congressman, John's accomplishments went beyond civil rights reform. He spoke up for better healthcare policies. He worked hard to improve education and fight poverty. John also helped protect the laws that the civil rights movement had fought to create. He oversaw renewals of the Voting Rights Act. His efforts improved the lives of both Black and white citizens in his district and beyond.

President Barack Obama awards the Presidential Medal of Freedom to Lewis.

At heart, John remained an activist. Even as a congressman, he participated in peaceful protests. He traveled to Africa to **renounce** human rights abuses such as segregation and the killing of innocent people. He protested quietly with others outside government buildings and was arrested many times. In the U.S., he led a peaceful sit-in on the House floor to persuade his peers to vote on gun control. He also spoke up when he did not agree with American presidents. His behavior won him the respect of his colleagues, including those who did not always agree with him. During his years in Congress, he received many awards for his activism efforts. In 2011, John was awarded the Presidential Medal of Freedom for his long civil rights career.

In 2019, John discovered he had cancer. Sadly, his wife had already passed away in 2012. He promised to keep working as long as he could. He continued to support others fighting for equal rights in America. Starting in 2013, the Black Lives Matter movement reminded many Americans that Black people were still fighting for their rights. The movement held many protests over the spring and early summer of 2020. While very ill, John followed their protests closely.

John Lewis wanted to share his passion for civil rights with young people. In 2013, Lewis and co-writer Andrew Aydin published *March*, the first of three graphic novels about his life as an activist. The award-winning trilogy was a huge success.

On July 17, 2020, John Lewis passed away. The great activist and politician was honored by people around the world. John Lewis had helped transform America into a place where African Americans and others who faced discrimination could speak up for their rights. He helped give people a voice, and those voices continue to fight for civil rights today.

Even after his death, the preacher had a few words to say. Just before he passed away, John asked the *New York Times* newspaper to publish a letter for him upon his death. In his letter, he encouraged young American activists to stand up for what they believed. "Walk with the wind, brothers and sisters," he wrote, "and let the spirit of peace and the power of everlasting love be your guide."

Lewis on the Edmund Pettus Bridge in Selma, Alabama, in 2015.

What should people know about John Lewis?
What is the importance of the work he did over the course of his lifetime?

What was the goal of the Freedom Riders?
What challenges did they face?
Do you think, given the chance, you would have been a Freedom Rider?

TIME LINE

1940-1959

1940
John Lewis is born on February 21 just outside Troy, Alabama.

1955
Lewis hears Dr. Martin Luther King Jr. on the radio for the first time. He is inspired to become an activist.

1957
Lewis moves to Nashville, Tennessee. He studies to become a minister at the American Baptist Theological Seminary. That same year, he joins the Nashville Student Movement.

1960

1960
Lewis participates in his first sit-in at a Nashville lunch counter. He is arrested for the first time. The sit-ins eventually lead to the first desegregation acts in the South when several lunch counters are desegregated.

1961
Lewis participates in the first Freedom Ride. He is savagely beaten and later arrested.

1963
Lewis becomes the chairman of the SNCC. He begins to plan the March on Washington with Dr. King and the other Big Six civil rights leaders. He gives his first public speech at this event.

1964
The U.S. government passes the Civil Rights Act, officially ending legal segregation.

1965
Lewis joins Dr. King and other protesters in a march from Selma to Montgomery, Alabama, in protest of African Americans' limited voting rights. John and other protesters are savagely beaten. The event known as "Bloody Sunday" leads to the passage of the Voting Rights Act one week later, enabling millions of African Americans to vote for the first time.

John left the SNCC when their methods became more aggressive.
Are peaceful protests the best way to bring about change?

Is there equality in the world today?
How does the answer to that question change depending on who you are?
Consider factors like a person's race, where they are from,
if they are rich or poor, male or female, etc.

| 1970-1989 | 2010 | 2020 |

1970
Lewis becomes the director of the Voter Education Project (VEP) and serves for 7 years.

1977
Lewis leaves the VEP to run for Congress. After he loses the election, President Carter names him director of the ACTION federal agency.

1981
Lewis is elected to public office for the first time as an Atlanta city councilman.

1986
Lewis is elected to the House of Representatives.

2011
Lewis receives the Presidential Medal of Freedom from President Obama.

2016
Lewis leads a sit-in on the House of Representatives floor after a mass shooting in Florida. He and other Congress members protest the government's lack of action on gun control.

2017
Lewis boycotts the inauguration of President Trump, stating that the president did not win a fair election.

2020
Lewis visits the Black Lives Matter Plaza in Washington, DC, named for the recent protests for African American rights. He is admitted to the hospital the next day and passes away from cancer on July 17 at the age of 80.

29

activist (AK-tih-vist)
An activist is someone who takes direct action for a particular cause. John Lewis was inspired to become an activist.

boycott (BOY-kot)
To boycott involves not using a certain product or service as a form of protest. In 1955, Dr. Martin Luther King Jr. led a boycott of the Montgomery bus system.

civil rights (SIV-il RITES)
Civil rights are personal freedoms that belong to all U.S. citizens. John Lewis dedicated his life to fighting for civil rights.

civil rights movement (SIV-il RITES MOOV-munt)
The civil rights movement is the name given to the struggle for equal rights for Black people in the United States during the 1950s and 1960s. John Lewis was a leader in the civil rights movement.

descendant (di-SEND-uhnt)
Descendants are someone's children, grandchildren, and so on. John Lewis was the descendant of slaves.

discrimination (diss-krim-ih-NAY-shun)
Discrimination is the unfair treatment of others based on things like race, gender, or age. John Lewis sought to fight discrimination against Black people.

ethnicity (eth-NIH-sih-tee)
A person's ethnicity is their cultural background. The Civil Rights Act of 1964 banned discrimination against anyone because of their ethnicity.

interracial (in-tur-RAY-shull)
When a group of people is interracial, the people in the group are from many different races.

literacy (LIT-ur-uh-see)
Literacy is the ability to read and write. In the past, Black people had to sometimes take literacy tests in order to vote.

races (RAY-sez)
Race is the idea of separating the world's people into groups. Oftentimes, races of people are constructed based on physical characteristics or social differences

racism (RAY-sih-zum)
Racism is the belief that one race is superior to another. John Lewis fought against racism.

renounce (reh-NOWNSS)
To renounce something is to refuse it very formally or publicly. John Lewis traveled to Africa to renounce segregation in that country.

resilience (reh-ZIL-yenss)
Resilience is the ability to recover from changes. When John Lewis was young, his preacher inspired him with messages of resilience.

segregated (SEG-reh-gay-ted)
If people or things are segregated, they are kept apart. Many places in the United States were once segregated, so African Americans either could not enter places or were kept separate from white people.

sharecroppers (SHAYR-krop-purz)
Sharecoppers are people who farm land in exchange for a portion of the crop's profits. John Lewis's parents were sharecroppers.

sit-ins (SIT-ins)
Sit-ins are a form of protest in which people enter a public place and refuse to leave for a long period of time. In 1960, students staged sit-ins to protest segregation at lunch counters.

sue (SOO)
When people sue other people, they take them to court to resolve a disagreement. Lewis wanted to sue Troy State College for discriminating against him because he was Black.

unconstitutional (un-kon-stih-TOO-shun-ull)
Something that is unconstitutional goes against the basic laws and principles of the U.S. Constitution. In 1946, the Supreme Court declared that segregation on interstate buses and trains was unconstitutional.

BOOKS

Asim, Jabari. *Preaching to the Chickens: The Story of Young John Lewis.*
New York, NY: Nancy Paulsen, 2016.

Doeden, Matt. *John Lewis: Courage in Action.* Minneapolis, MN: Lerner, 2018.

Haskins, James and Kathleen Benson. *The Story of Civil Rights Hero
John Lewis.* New York, NY: Lee & Low Books, 2018.

Leslie, Tonya. *The Story of John Lewis.* Emeryville, CA: Rockridge Press, 2021.

Pinkney, Andrea Davis. *Because of You, John Lewis.* New York, NY: Scholastic, 2021.

WEBSITES

Visit our website for links about John Lewis:

childsworld.com/links

*Note to Parents, Teachers, and Librarians: We routinely verify our Web links to make sure
they are safe, active sites—so encourage your readers to check them out!*

INDEX